A return to Head Covering

A Needed Symbol in the Contemporary Church

by Dr. Carlton C. McLeod

† CCMCLEOD
† MINISTRIES
SOLA SCRIPTURA

Chesapeake, Virginia

First Printing: May 2017

Cover art and typography by Justin Turley.

Printed in the United States of America.

*To all my Brothers and Sisters in
Christ who will disagree. . .
grace, honor, love, and peace.*

Table of Contents

Preface—
The Pain & the Privilege

But he answered and said, "It is written, Man shall not live by bread alone, but by every word that proceedeth out of the mouth of God." (Matthew 4:4)

In January 2013, the LORD prompted me to teach through the *Epistle of First Corinthians*, line by line. Knowing what was in this Pauline letter to the church at Corinth, I was excited, but nervous. Why? Because of the implications of actually being obedient to what was written therein. In fact, I "double-checked" with the LORD in prayer in an attempt to discern if this was in fact His will for our congregation. I asked the other elders. We talked about it and prayed. Why all this consternation? Because First Corinthians is a scary book; other parts of Scripture would have been much easier! In May of 2013, we prayerfully began, finishing in December, 2014.

Well, I can say my fears were founded. The Epistle shook our church. Why? Because we refused to simply ignore or explain away tough passages and actually worked our way through them in context as best we could. As a result, we upset people. We lost some people. I was and have continued to be subject to increased criticism. Again… why? Because this section of Holy Scripture contains many things people in the modern era do not like, particularly in the areas of church discipline, gifts, church order, and women's issues. That is the bottom line.

In particular, 1 Corinthians 11:1-16 was exceptionally challenging. I did the best I could to explain the Text, in the historical context, and even took the time to demonstrate how the church throughout history responded to this holy ordinance. Nevertheless, it was difficult for many women in our congregation to hear. Some left our church. Most never said it was over the head coverings sermon, but I knew. On the bright side, a small but increasing number began to cover. Others have covered, and stopped, and started, and stopped, and started… Our men continue uniformly NOT covering. ☺

Now an admission: I fought personal bias concerning this ordinance, and only overcame them after months of study. When I was forced to be honest with this Text, it all suddenly made sense. However, I must confess that I didn't really understand how the head covering verses would affect our wonderful ladies. As a man, I just didn't get it. Wrestling with shame? Dealing with embarrassment? Different fashion choices? Modesty issues? Having to process one's self-image? Having to fight against feminist indoctrination? The whole "hair" subject in general? Submission to male authority? All these things and more were rolled into a piece of cloth on the head during times of prayer and prophecy.

We worked hard to make sure no one felt judged. Some did anyway, which is heartbreaking. I suppose the visible nature of the symbol kind of causes that. With as much love and grace as we could muster, all the ladies were given a choice to cover or not based on their family's decision, but it has been hard to move on. Literally it has taken us a few years to recover.

On a much happier note, our church is also stronger. We gained people too, people who loved the fact that we stood on Scripture. People heard about our church and visited from far and wide. We deepened our faith. We took these apostolic directives seriously, and God has "blessed us in the doing!" (Jam 1:25) Yes, it looks and feels a little odd...a church that is attempting to apply biblical directives without compromise in 2017. We make tons of mistakes LORD knows, but we are trying. Thank you, Jesus, for grace! ☺

The ordinance of head covering does indeed challenge the all-too-often man-centered modern church, and that in my opinion is a good thing. The American church is suffering now in part, because we refuse to take God at His Word. In fact, I believe the church has lost her *prophetic voice*...her willingness to declare "what thus says the LORD," and the entire world is hurting as a result.

By God's grace, my sermon on head covering, which was posted on the popular blog, *The Head Covering Movement*[1] has been viewed thousands of times around the world. I've received and continue to receive emails and phones calls from all over the Nation and countries in Europe and Asia. Apparently, God is moving segments of the church back to this Spirit-ordained practice. I've included some of the more encouraging comments in this book.

Without a doubt, 1 Corinthians brought some *pain*. But I'd be remiss if I didn't declare that it was indeed a *privilege* to hear what thus says the LORD in this Epistle, and do our very best to obey Him, regardless of the cost.

Soli Deo Gloria!

---

1. HeadCoveringMovement.com/biblical-sermons/head-coverings-history-context-and-exegesis-sermon

The Eve Controversy

Unto the woman he said, I will greatly multiply thy sorrow and thy conception; in sorrow thou shalt bring forth children; and thy desire shall be to thy husband, and he shall rule over thee. (Genesis 3:16)

During the recent Presidential election cycle, my wife and I watched part of one of the debates. I hadn't watched a full political debate the entire election season. We watched the debate in which the question was whether women should be forced to register for Selective Service when they turn 18 (as must men). Selective Service, historically, is used when our Nation must draft people to fight in the armed forces.

And we heard, in our opinion (which prayerfully, is informed by the Bible) some VERY shaky answers.

I made this statement in the opening of a recent sermon on the *Value and Sanctity of Human Life*...

Every Woman's Issue Is Controversial

Friends, it's true. From her hair to keeping her home, her modesty to her meek and quiet manner, her being under headship to her head covering, it really is true. Should she have children? How many? Should she work outside the home? Should she homeschool? Should she be able to abort her own children? Should she lead men in the church? Should she take her husband's last name? Is keeping a home still important? Should she dress modestly or are yoga pants in public ok? Should she be able to be a SEAL or Army Ranger? The President? An Elder or Bishop? The household breadwinner on purpose (the man voluntarily staying home while she works, not due to a job loss, etc.)? You name it, and if it is a woman's issue, there is controversy surrounding it today, both in the church and without.

Now hear me. I'm not throwing stones or judging. This is simply true. Everything about who she is and what she should or should not do is discussed, dissected, and disputed!

By contrast, most (at least in the church) still agree on men's issues. Most believe he should work outside the home. Most still agree he is responsible for providing in some context. Most still agree he's supposed to be a warrior, both spiritually and literally... at 2am during a bump in the night or on a battlefield in a hostile country. Most still agree he's supposed to lead at least in some way.

But for the precious daughters of Eve, things are not so simple. False ideas about womanhood are **promoted** by feminism. True womanhood is **perverted** by false belief systems. The whole subject of womanhood in general **petrifies** the Church! Petrifies the church? Yes! I've seen many a pastor innocently wade into the womanhood waters only to poke a hornet's nest. Yet in light of the influence (more like the takeover) of feminism (where God-designed distinctions between the sexes are shunned) and the perversions of Islam in our day (where women are treated horribly, like property), **the Church has a marvelous opportunity!**

> *The Church can display for the whole world, God's loving design for women! God wants women honored and protected! Although God gave her a different role to play, she is a joint-heir with men in Christ! Scripture shows that motherhood is beautiful! By divine design, her role as a helper is critical! Femininity as displayed in Scripture, reflects a heavenly vision! A godly woman is strong and confident in her LORD and what He has commanded of her!*

If Scripture is God's loving heart towards His people, and if Christ and His Gospel are the only proper lenses through which we must see the world, then we find that Biblical Womanhood is not only beautiful, but is unveiled and affirmed by God. If we look only to Scripture, we can see clearly what God wants for His beloved daughters, and everything about that is beautiful.

The Question Is: "Will We Look to the Bible, and Look Honestly?"

As we approach this "hot" topic together, may we look to the Bible, and look earnestly. May the LORD's Word burn within our hearts as He helps us understand what He taught us (Lk 24:32), and may His Anointing still teach us (1 Jn 2:27).

For the record, my wife and I DO NOT want our daughters registering for Selective Service, nor do we want them forward deployed in the sandbox with an M16 in full battle rattle.

Don't judge us!

Reading
1 Corinthians 11:1-16

All scripture is given by inspiration of God, and is profitable for doctrine, for reproof, for correction, for instruction in righteousness: That the man of God may be perfect, throughly furnished unto all good works. (2 Timothy 3:16-17)

King James Version, Verse by Verse

1. Be ye followers of me, even as I also am of Christ.
2. Now I praise you, brethren, that ye remember me in all things, and keep the ordinances, as I delivered them to you.
3. But I would have you know, that the head of every man is Christ; and the head of the woman is the man; and the head of Christ is God.
4. Every man praying or prophesying, having his head covered, dishonoureth his head.

5. But every woman that prayeth or prophesieth with her head uncovered dishonoureth her head: for that is even all one as if she were shaven.

6. For if the woman be not covered, let her also be shorn: but if it be a shame for a woman to be shorn or shaven, let her be covered.

7. For a man indeed ought not to cover his head, forasmuch as he is the image and glory of God: but the woman is the glory of the man.

8. For the man is not of the woman; but the woman of the man.

9. Neither was the man created for the woman; but the woman for the man.

10. For this cause ought the woman to have power on her head because of the angels.

11. Nevertheless neither is the man without the woman, neither the woman without the man, in the LORD.

12. For as the woman is of the man, even so is the man also by the woman; but all things of God.

13. Judge in yourselves: is it comely that a woman pray unto God uncovered?

14. Doth not even nature itself teach you, that, if a man have long hair, it is a shame unto him?

15. But if a woman have long hair, it is a glory to her: for her hair is given her for a covering.

16. But if any man seem to be contentious, we have no such custom, neither the churches of God.

English Standard Version (ESV), Verse by Verse

1. Be imitators of me, as I am of Christ.
2. Now I commend you because you remember me in everything and maintain the traditions even as I delivered them to you.
3. But I want you to understand that the head of every man is Christ, the head of a wife is her husband, and the head of Christ is God.
4. Every man who prays or prophesies with his head covered dishonors his head,
5. but every wife who prays or prophesies with her head uncovered dishonors her head, since it is the same as if her head were shaven.
6. For if a wife will not cover her head, then she should cut her hair short. But since it is disgraceful for a wife to cut off her hair or shave her head, let her cover her head.
7. For a man ought not to cover his head, since he is the image and glory of God, but woman is the glory of man.
8. For man was not made from woman, but woman from man.
9. Neither was man created for woman, but woman for man.
10. That is why a wife ought to have a symbol of authority on her head, because of the angels.
11. Nevertheless, in the LORD woman is not independent of man nor man of woman;

12. for as woman was made from man, so man is now born of woman. And all things are from God.
13. Judge for yourselves: is it proper for a wife to pray to God with her head uncovered?
14. Does not nature itself teach you that if a man wears long hair it is a disgrace for him,
15. but if a woman has long hair, it is her glory? For her hair is given to her for a covering.
16. If anyone is inclined to be contentious, we have no such practice, nor do the churches of God.

A Word about "Wives" vs. "Women"

These two popular Bible translations translate the Greek word *gunē* differently. The KJV renders the word *women* while the ESV translates it as *wives*. This is almost totally an extra-biblical opinion on the part of the ESV translators. I enjoy and use the ESV, but I think their considerations were based in some level on bias against the practice described. Indeed, the popular *ESV Study Bible* says on verse three:

> *Since a woman's head covering in first-century Roman society was a sign of marriage, Paul's practical concern in this passage is not with the relationship between women and men generally but with the relationship between husband and wife.*

In my opinion, this interpretation is read into Scripture and is foreign to the reasons the Holy Spirit actually gives for the practice of head covering through the Apostle Paul.

Although I believe the passages apply to wives, I also think they carry a broader application for single women as well. A single woman still has a head (her literal physical head, representing her own humility and shamefacedness before God, her father, her elders, and of course, Christ Himself, who gets to decide how He is approached in worship).

Just as single men should not cover during times of prayer and prophecy (the example that gives most an "aha moment" on this issue) because they still must honor Christ, likewise the single woman should maintain this ordinance as well. Every pastor I know would kindly ask a man of any marital status to remove his hat when entering into a worship service. To that I say, "Amen."

History, Context, & Exegesis

Whom shall he teach knowledge? and whom shall he make to understand doctrine? them that are weaned from the milk, and drawn from the breasts. For precept must be upon precept, precept upon precept; line upon line, line upon line; here a little, and there a little. (Isaiah 28:9-10)

History

So again, have you ever wondered why men remove their hats when they pray or come into a sanctuary, or many times when they go inside a home? Have you ever wondered why a woman veils herself during her wedding? I think these are fair questions. The truth is the church DOES practice head covering each Sunday… for men only.

Obviously, it is NOT a sin for a woman to wear a head covering, either in worship or in public. The question is not whether it is a sin TO wear one, but whether it is a sin to NOT wear one. I suppose that depends on whether or not we believe that what Paul wrote were "commandments of the LORD." (1 Cor 14:37)

If the history of the church is any guide, it is a fact that from the time of the Apostles until approximately the mid 20th Century, Christian women covered their heads in worship, and many times in public as well, while Christian men did not. Look at the following quotes.

The Early Church & Head Coverings

"The oral and written history handed down to us from the early Church is an example in these matters; we can look to the practical way they obeyed this command... In the second century, Hippolytus of Rome wrote the Apostolic Tradition—a collection of the customs of the early Church. It includes the statement "let all the women have their heads covered." Furthermore, the catacombs (a system of burial caverns under Rome where early Christians hid during times of persecution), are full of pictures of women praying with coverings and men without. Not only was it an apostolic teaching, but various early church fathers such as Augustine of Hippo, Saint John Chrysostom, Tertullian and others taught and encouraged it. John Calvin and Matthew Henry both taught and practiced the tradition of head coverings, and the Protestant

reformer Martin Luther's wife wore one. John Wesley taught it as well."[1]

American History: Head Coverings

"During the nineteenth century, many Christians in the United States and western Europe began arguing that long hair constituted the only covering women needed. Others said that women only needed to wear a covering when in church. The middle class and wealthy women switched from veils and caps to ornate bonnets if they wore a covering at all. Bonnets became more a matter of fashion than of modesty or obedience to 1 Corinthians 11. By the turn of the twentieth century, the ornate bonnets of the nineteenth century had given way to ladies' hats. Until the mid-century, women in Europe and America typically wore a hat or scarf in public, but they were simply following tradition and fashion without realizing that there was originally a spiritual reason behind the practice. Similarly, until about 1960, western women wore hats when in church. But the meaning behind the hat was lost."[2]

---

1. (Yohannan, K.P. *Head Coverings: What the Bible Teaches about Head Coverings for Women.* Believers Church Publications, 2011. Print.)

2. (Bercot, David. "Head Covering Through the Centuries." Scroll Publishing, n.d. Web. 27 August 2013.) One can even find pictures online of women wearing head coverings over the centuries. Here is a good place to start: www.scrollpublishing.com/store/head-covering-history.html

So from Paul's time and the earliest church meetings until very recently, this passage that is so controversial (or ignored) in the modern church wasn't so at all. Other than maybe the bit about angels, 1 Corinthians 11 was obvious and easy to understand for Christians of all denominations, cultures, and ethnicities. Women/wives were supposed to cover their heads, at least when they approached God, because God said so. It is no longer so easy. Literally, churches have split and much damage has been done right here in 1 Corinthians 11… over a little bit of fabric on the head and more to the point, what it symbolizes.

Culture?

Now to be sure, head coverings is a second tier doctrine. Heaven or hell doesn't hang in the balance. It doesn't rise to the importance of the triune nature of God, the deity of Christ, or the Gospel. But it is included in the Canon of Scripture and is no less inspired than any other part of the Bible.

The question for us is really one of what to do with culture. Are we simply dealing with a symbol (a head covering) that has lost its significance today so another symbol (like a wedding ring), or just a wife's attitude would suffice? Many say this issue is one of a wife's submission… the symbol used isn't that important. Such esteemed evangelical leaders as Wayne Grudem and John MacArthur take this position.

This subject is made all the more difficult because very, very few Christian women in the West wear head coverings anymore. Not coincidentally in my opinion, the widespread jettisoning of this practice can be traced to the mid-Twentieth Century, right around the rise of modern feminism. Many influenced by feminist ideology would not only see marriage as "a comfortable concentration camp," (quote from Betty Friedan, founder of N.O.W.) but abhor ANY symbols of a women being under authority.

And this leads me to my concern and caution: current church tendency is to NOT see Scripture as sufficient, and when faced with a counter-cultural passage is quick to say it no longer applies for the sake of cultural norms. For example:

- The Bible takes a dim view of debt? So what! *We don't live that way anymore... debt is great!*
- The Bible says husbands lovingly lead their homes and wives walk in submission? *We don't live in 1950!*
- The Bible says women shouldn't lead in the church and preach? *Paul was a chauvinist! There were uneducated Amazons in Ephesus!*
- The Bible declares homosexuality an abominable sin? *They were talking about sexual assaults and didn't understand "orientation." C'mon now... love is love!*

So often, we say of plain, obvious Scriptures, "I know it says that but it doesn't mean that." The danger is once everything becomes "that was then, this is now; it no longer applies," all standards get thrown out. Marriage, family, the meaning of the Gospel, the concept of sin and what is lawful or not... even the concept of grace can be distorted. Dear reader, I have a healthy fear of the LORD and of tampering with His Word. I pray you do as well!

Ye shall not add unto the word which I command you, neither shall ye diminish ought from it, that ye may keep the commandments of the LORD your God which I command you. (Deuteronomy 4:2)

For I testify unto every man that heareth the words of the prophecy of this book, If any man shall add unto these things, God shall add unto him the plagues that are written in this book: And if any man shall take away from the words of the book of this prophecy, God shall take away his part out of the book of life, and out of the holy city, and from the things which are written in this book. He which testifieth these things saith, Surely I come quickly. Amen. Even so, come, LORD *Jesus. (Revelation 22:18-20)*

And let us recall that:

All scripture is given by inspiration of God, and is profitable for doctrine, for reproof, for correction, for instruction in righteousness: That the man of God may be perfect, throughly furnished unto all good works. (2 Timothy 3:16-17)

Some Thoughts on Context

Many believers who hold to head covering see this passage as primarily dealing with church meetings. Why? Because prayer and prophecy are mentioned in verses 4-5, and prayer might be private at times, but prophecy is designed for the Body (1 Cor 14:3). Others see it as broader than that, viewing the command as relevant whenever men and women pray and prophesy. This view seems to be confirmed later in the chapter when Paul begins to address the worship gathering specifically:

> *Now in this that I declare unto you I praise you not, that ye come together not for the better, but for the worse. For first of all, when ye come together in the church, I hear that there be divisions among you; and I partly believe it. (1 Corinthians 11:17-18)*

Both groups agree, however, that whatever we learn about head coverings certainly would apply in LORD's Day worship.

But there is another contextual consideration that is important exegetically for another reason. Many people use 1 Corinthians 11 to essentially throw out New Testament commands concerning women's roles within the church. They generally teach that "since a woman can pray and prophesy in worship" she can also preach and be a pastor. But as John Calvin wrote in his commentaries:

> *For when he reproves them for prophesying with their head uncovered, he at the same time does not give them permission to prophesy in some other*

way, but delays his condemnation of that vice until another passage, namely 1 Corinthians 14.

The passage Calvin is referencing states:

> *For God is not the author of confusion, but of peace, as in all churches of the saints. Let your women keep silence in the churches: for it is not permitted unto them to speak; but they are commanded to be under obedience, as also saith the law. And if they will learn any thing, let them ask their husbands at home: for it is a shame for women to speak in the church. What? came the word of God out from you? or came it unto you only? If any man think himself to be a prophet, or spiritual, let him acknowledge that the things that I write unto you are the commandments of the LORD. But if any man be ignorant, let him be ignorant. (1 Corinthians 14:33–38)*

These verses would seem to contradict 1 Corinthians 11 if women could publicly pray and prophesy in church services as opposed to elsewhere in a context fitting to her design and God-ordained role. The Bible does not contradict itself.

In the 1st Century and early church, we can be reasonably certain that:

1. Women/wives covered their heads when they prayed or prophesied.
2. Women/wives were covered in church services.
3. Any prayer or prophecy by women was done in such a way as to not be "shameful" in the churches.

Exegesis

1 Corinthians 11:2

> *Now I praise you, brethren, that ye remember me in all things, and keep the ordinances, as I delivered them to you.*

There are two uses in the New Testament for the word *paradosis* in Greek, translated as "traditions." One means something man-made that attempts to invalidate what is handed down by God (Matt 15:3), and the other is literally a precept... something that IS in fact handed down by God. Here are two examples of the latter:

> *Therefore, brethren, stand fast, and hold the <u>traditions</u> which ye have been taught, whether by word, or our epistle. (2 Thessalonians 2:15)*

> *Now we command you, brethren, in the name of our LORD Jesus Christ, that ye withdraw yourselves from every brother that walketh disorderly, and not after the <u>tradition</u> which he received of us. (2 Thessalonians 3:6)*

It seems fairly evident that in 1 Corinthians 11:2, the word implies in context, a precept, or as the KJV translates it... an *ordinance*... a liturgical law. Paul's language throughout this lengthy section of Scripture makes clear that this was no "take it or leave it" thing for the early "churches of God."

(v16) Every church practiced it, and it was dishonorable for a man to be covered and a woman to be uncovered.

1 Corinthians 11:3

But I would have you know, that the head of every man is Christ; and the head of the woman is the man; and the head of Christ is God.

- After a quick commendation, Paul begins to build a case for the "tradition" or ordinance of head covering. The context of the entire passage indicates there may have been some attempt to adhere to this ordinance, but further obedience was needed.
- Verse three is an unequivocal statement of God's *Governing Order.* It is important to see that this truth is not based in culture. It was and is true and binding for all time.
- Contrary to egalitarian opinion, the word "head" doesn't mean "source." It means "one who is in authority over."
- It is also important to note that this does not imply inferiority, but role. Christ is not inferior to the Father... they are one! However, He is subordinate to the Father within the Trinity. Similarly, women/wives (Greek, gunē, which again can be translated "wife" or "woman" depending on context) is not inferior to man; she is designed by God as a helper (Gen 2:18) and therefore submits to her husband.

1 Corinthians 11:4

Every man praying or prophesying, having his head covered, dishonoureth his head.

- As we'll see below, because man is the glory of God (which means he was formed by God first out of the dust of the ground, Gen 2:7), he is not to be covered when he prays or prophesies. Again, please note that this instruction is rooted in God's governing order.
- According to Scripture, when a man covers his head in worship he dishonors Christ, his Head!
- Man's physical, uncovered head is a symbolic way <u>God has chosen</u> to reveal His own glory in the church, since man is made in His image.
- Of note, women are also made in God's image, but again, with a different role.
- Let's establish that symbols, at least to God, are important. What are Baptism and the LORD's Supper if not physical symbols that represent deeper, spiritual realities? And let us not forget the symbol of the blood on the doorposts during the Passover (Exodus 12). Did the death angel "need" a physical symbol to know who belonged to God? Either way, a symbol (the blood) was commanded at the risk of death.

1 Corinthians 11:5

But every woman that prayeth or prophesieth with her head uncovered dishonoureth her head: for that is even all one as if she were shaven.

- Since a man needed to be uncovered, a woman needed to be distinct and be covered. There is no androgyny in the Bible!
- Really understand what Paul is saying here. Apparently, some Corinthian men wanted to be covered (a Jewish tradition) and some Corinthian women wanted to be uncovered, which in the sight of God would have been shameful.
- Paul is saying that a man is in rebellion against his head (Christ) by covering, and a woman is in rebellion against her head (her own standing before God, the authority over her, like her husband, father, etc., or ultimately Christ Himself) by uncovering during times of prayer and prophesying, or worship.
- The word for cover in these verses (vv3-6) in Greek (katakaluptō) is a word that means *to be veiled or unveiled.* This was, based on grammar, context, and history, a literal, physical, material covering.

1 Corinthians 11:6

For if the woman be not covered, let her also be shorn: but if it be a shame for a woman to be shorn or shaven, let her be covered.

- We see two conditions presented here: to be shaved (shorn) or to be covered. They are obviously two different states. This is important because many today believe that the head covering is hair. It is not. If a woman will not cover, Paul says she should shave off her hair.

- It is clear though that such an act (shaving the hair off) is not Paul's intention. He was simply pointing out how a purposely uncovered head is just as shameful as a purposely shaved head.
- The divine hierarchy apparently needed to be reestablished in Corinth, especially since it was taught in all the churches (v16). This hierarchy was to be reinforced visually.
- Paul's language here (*shame* in the KJV, or *disgraceful* in the ESV) leaves little room for argument. At least to Paul, this wasn't a small matter.

1 Corinthians 11:7

For a man indeed ought not to cover his head, forasmuch as he is the image and glory of God: but the woman is the glory of the man.

- This passage points us back to Genesis. Paul uses *Creation Order* as part of his defense of head coverings.
- As we've already said, both male and female are made in God's image (Gen 1:27), but woman was given another part to play. Just as man is God's glory, she is man's glory.
- According to Scripture, even before the Fall, *woman was created for the man (Gen 2:20), from the man (Gen 2:21), brought to the man (Gen 2:22), and named by the man (Gen 2:23).* I know this sounds horrible to many modern ears; it just happens to be true!
- And woman is beautiful! She is man's glory! God's

design is perfect! She isn't inferior; she is created with divine purpose!

- However, in worship, her glory must be veiled, that only God's glory shows. For a woman to be uncovered or to otherwise flaunt herself was to cast off the authority over her, place herself in man's place, be immodest, and promote man's glory.

1 Corinthians 11:8

For the man is not of the woman; but the woman of the man.

- Again, Paul uses *Creation Order* for his defense of head coverings and both a man's and a woman's role within the church.
- This is similar to Paul's reasoning in 1 Timothy 2: *Let the woman learn in silence with all subjection. But I suffer not a woman to teach, nor to usurp authority over the man, but to be in silence. For Adam was first formed, then Eve. And Adam was not deceived, but the woman being deceived was in the transgression. (1 Timothy 2:11-14)*

1 Corinthians 11:9

Neither was the man created for the woman; but the woman for the man.

- This is more commentary on the Genesis account. Eve was created for Adam, to be a helper fit for him. It was not good for Adam to be alone.

1 Corinthians 11:10

For this cause ought the woman to have power on her head because of the angels.

- So then God's *Governing Order* and *Creation Order* serve as foundations for why a woman ought to have power (or "a symbol of authority" ESV) on her head.
- This phrase, "power on her head," has been subject to two main interpretations. The Greek word for *power* is *exousia*, and means "authority." There is a debate around the question: "Is the authority her own, or another's, like her husband or father?"
- A third view is that the head covering does symbolize a *husband's* authority and may also symbolize a woman's *personal* authority as a believer to pray unto God, but is also a symbol to spiritual forces that she is *under* authority, created for men, not angels. (See the "Because of the Angels" chapter.)
- Although I'm not dogmatic about it, this is the view I hold and it fits the context. The head covering may be a tool for spiritual warfare, a realm in which we lean fully on Christ and the power of what He has commanded.
- Regardless of one's position on *exousia* however, for most of Christian history, the symbol of a woman's submission and a woman's understanding and embracing of her role was a head covering... something literal and physical on her head.
- Paul teaches an additional reason for the covering: "*Because of the Angels.*"

- There are many interpretations here. The most popular is the view that angels, as ministering spirits who perfectly obey God's commands and order, are present as we worship and would be offended at any disregard of God's design and will. Also, Satan and all demons, who fell because of rebellion and pride (Isa 14:13-14), would be publicly rebuked by this symbol of order and obedience.

- There is wonderful merit in this view. I'll humbly offer another, more involved take on this in a later chapter. It is however noteworthy that even mighty angels cover parts of themselves in the presence of God:

  In the year that king Uzziah died I saw also the LORD sitting upon a throne, high and lifted up, and his train filled the temple. Above it stood the seraphims: each one had six wings; with twain he covered his face, and with twain he covered his feet, and with twain he did fly. And one cried unto another, and said, Holy, holy, holy, is the LORD of hosts: the whole earth is full of his glory. (Isaiah 6:1-3)

- Here is a critical thought: whatever "because of the angels" means, it is very unlikely that the meaning was unique to first century Corinthians. As I taught my church when I preached this, "angels ain't cultural."

- The hated symbol of head covering is, in my opinion, a rebuke to today's sexually confused society. The church is supposed to model God's order! And yet, even in the church, roles are reversing as we surrender more and more to man's perversity and opinion. But American culture is not alone. Many other cultures are also confused about the sexes. Holding up "culture" as a standard is a losing game. We must look to Scripture!

1 Corinthians 11:11

Nevertheless neither is the man without the woman, neither the woman without the man, in the LORD.

- Lest any man think he can take sinful advantage of his position as leader by mistreating his wife (or any women for that matter), Paul speaks this truth: we are interdependent. Man needs woman and woman needs man.

1 Corinthians 11:12

For as the woman is of the man, even so is the man also by the woman; but all things of God.

- Again, men and women are heirs together in Christ (1 Pet 3:7), but with differing roles. We must not confuse role/order differences with intrinsic value before the LORD.

1 Corinthians 11:13

Judge in yourselves: is it comely that a woman pray unto God uncovered?

- This is a rhetorical question. Based on everything Paul has said to this point, the answer is obviously "no." Therefore he calls this church to consider his teaching, using their common sense and knowledge of God.
- The word comely means *suitable* or *proper*. Is it proper for a woman to approach God uncovered? No.

1 Corinthians 11:14

Doth not even nature itself teach you, that, if a man have long hair, it is a shame unto him?

- Another part of Paul's defense of head coverings is *Nature*. God's natural design of men and women speaks to the need for the man to be uncovered and the woman to be covered during prayer.
- He appeals to men looking like men and women looking like women...a natural, normal thing that shows differences in divine design. For a man to look like a woman in the church is a "shame unto him."

1 Corinthians 11:15

But if a woman have long hair, it is a glory to her: for her hair is given her for a covering.

- Some say a woman's hair is her covering and that no other is needed. But the word here for covering is different in the Greek than in verses 3-6. I've included an entire chapter on this issue, but it is reasonably apparent that if a woman's hair is her symbolic covering, none of this argument would have even been necessary in the first place (since most women have hair, and longer hair than men!). Paul must have lost his mind, fussing over nothing!

- There has been no evidence found that Christian women in Corinth were running around with shaved heads. But even if "there were women on the Island of Lesbos with shaved heads acting like men," we must be careful. Exegetically, Paul does not mention anything of the sort. He mentions Genesis. He mentions Angels. Every church obeyed the ordinance, not just the church in Corinth.
- Mentioning a woman's hair was the Spirit's way of giving His people an example from *Nature*: women are naturally covered (longer hair) and men are not (shorter hair). This reality demonstrates women should also be symbolically covered.
- Although it is not the main point, it was also a way of affirming modesty in worship. A woman's hair is her glory. To cover her head is to veil part of that which sets her apart as glorious.

1 Corinthians 11:16

But if any man seem to be contentious, we have no such custom, neither the churches of God.

- Paul ends his defense of head coverings by appealing to *Normative Church Practice*. Essentially, he's saying that if anyone wants to keep arguing about this, they should not. All the churches of God (not just Corinth) practiced the head covering.

- There was "no such custom" as disregarding the ordinance of head coverings. History bears out Paul's point quite convincingly concerning the uniformity of the practice of "the churches of God," right up until modern times.

Conclusions

1. The biblical ordinance of head covering is rooted in *God's Government, Creation Order, Angelic Observance, Creation itself (Nature), and Normative Church Practice.*

2. Symbols are important as visible, outward signs of internal realities (The LORD's Supper and Baptism as examples).

3. Although many hold to a cultural hermeneutic, it is hard to make that case from Scripture alone, especially since eternal and spiritual reasons for the practice are given by Paul in the Text.

4. As a result of 1 Corinthians 11:1-16, which is actually reasonably straightforward, Christian women (not just wives) covered their heads during worship for the entire history of the church until very recently, and many in the world still do.

5. We therefore believe the practice (for both men and women) is a biblical ordinance, and is just as relevant today as it was in the first century A.D.

"Because of the Angels"
Head Coverings
& Spiritual Warfare

Are they not all ministering spirits, sent forth to minister for them who shall be heirs of salvation? (Hebrews 1:14)

Let us look again at our text, specifically at verses 9-10:

*Neither was the man created for the woman; **but the woman for the man**. **For this cause** ought the woman to have power on her head because of the angels. (1 Corinthians 11:9-10, KJV)*

Consider the phrase: "For this cause." For what cause? The answer in context is *the woman being created for the man.* Scripture declares:

*And the LORD God said, It is not good that the man should be alone; **I will make him an help meet for him**. (Gen 2:18)*

And Adam gave names to all cattle, and to the fowl of the air, and to every beast of the field; **but for Adam there was not found an help meet for him.** *And the LORD God caused a deep sleep to fall upon Adam, and he slept: and he took one of his ribs, and closed up the flesh instead thereof;* **And the rib, which the LORD God had taken from man, made he a woman, and brought her unto the man.** *And Adam said, This is now bone of my bones, and flesh of my flesh: she shall be called Woman, because she was taken out of Man. Therefore shall a man leave his father and his mother, and shall cleave unto his wife: and they shall be one flesh. (Gen 2:20-24)*

An Exegetical Question

Why is "power" (or a "symbol of authority", ESV) needed on a woman's head "because of the angels" as a result of her being created for the man?

Let us think this through. What interactions do we read about in Scripture where angels would need to know, be reminded of, or see a demonstration of this truth: *the woman was created for the man*? Two possibilities come to mind:

1. Eve and Satan in the garden
2. The "sons of God" taking attractive women as wives in Genesis 6:1-6

The latter, if taken at face value, would make a great deal of sense. The angels in Genesis 6 actually took women for themselves and engaged in unholy marriage and physical perversions with them. This abomination was contrary to God's design. Human women are made for human men! (1 Cor 11:8-9) However, the former is instructive as well. Note who Satan went to in the garden!

Perhaps the head covering is needed not only for the other reasons Paul mentions in 1 Cor 11 (creation order, governing order, nature, church conformity), but also to remind all angels present in the midst of worship that women are for men and not them, veiling their beauty (which attracted the angels) in the process.

I missed this completely in the past, partially because I had been hesitant to take Genesis 6:1-6 as written:

1. And it came to pass, when men began to multiply on the face of the earth, and daughters were born unto them,
2. That the sons of God saw the daughters of men that they were fair; and they took them wives of all which they chose.
3. And the LORD said, My spirit shall not always strive with man, for that he also is flesh: yet his days shall be an hundred and twenty years.
4. There were giants in the earth in those days; and also after that, when the sons of God came in unto the daughters of men, and they bare children to them, the same became mighty men which were of old, men of renown.

5. And GOD saw that the wickedness of man was great in the earth, and that every imagination of the thoughts of his heart was only evil continually.
6. And it repented the LORD that he had made man on the earth, and it grieved him at his heart.

The term "sons of God" is normally an angelic term in the Old Testament (Job 1:6, 2:1, 38:7). In context the term almost certainly means angelic beings (as opposed to human messengers), given the distinction between this term and the "daughters of men." Genesis 6:4-5 give the reasons for the Flood: in addition to man's depravity, the sons of God procreating with the daughters of men was something so wicked that God decided to destroy all living things on land.

If this view is true, *here we have a cataclysmic interaction between women and angels where angels left the order and design of God.* They lusted after "fair" women, drawn apparently by their beauty. Certainly, the head covering may also teach "good" angels something about divine order or a woman's submission to her husband/father/ elders. But the tenor and tone of 1 Cor 11:10 seems to imply something defensive. Perhaps it says to angelic observers of all types (Heb 1:14), "she belongs to man, not you." Given the events in Genesis 6, she therefore covers her "glory" (herself, 1 Cor 11:7, and her hair, 1 Cor 11:15), veiling her beauty from the angels (drawn to our worship) in submission to and protected by the authority over her. In this scenario, one would think both married and single women would want such powerful protection...

For we wrestle not against flesh and blood, but against principalities, against powers, against the rulers of the darkness of this world, against spiritual wickedness in high places. (Eph 6:12)

This forces one to wonder about the church's susceptibility to demonic attack during prayer and prophecy (this would include worship) when the head covering teachings aren't observed. Although many call the head covering a "small thing" (and compared to the Gospel it surely is), perhaps our rejection of this ordinance promotes the current sensuality, rebellion, immodesty, powerlessness, perversions, usurpations of male authority, homosexuality, and general lack of holiness and reverence tolerated and sometimes even celebrated in the modern church.

Amazingly, the head covering may actually be a defensive tool during spiritual warfare! If my interpretation has merit, it is also a rebuke to the angels who fell into lust. I believe the Genesis 6 angels are who Peter and Jude are speaking about:

For if God spared not the angels that sinned, but cast them down to hell, and delivered them into chains of darkness, to be reserved unto judgment; And spared not the old world, but saved Noah the eighth person, a preacher of righteousness, bringing in the flood upon the world of the ungodly; (2 Peter 2:4-5)

And the angels which kept not their first estate, but left their own habitation, he hath reserved in everlasting chains under darkness unto the judgment of the great day. Even as Sodom and Gomorrah, and the cities about them in like manner, giving themselves over to fornication, and going after strange flesh, are set forth for an example, suffering the vengeance of eternal fire. (Jude 1:6-7)

Based on his reference to the Flood, Peter seems to be referring to Genesis 6. If so, and since both verses four and five are in the same context, he establishes for us that the "angels" in view are not a line of humans, but heavenly angels.

Jude 7 says "Even as" and "in like manner." I believe this means "in like manner" to the angels mentioned in Jude 6. In other words, the sin of Sodom and Gomorrah and the surrounding cities was similar to the sin of the angels in Jude 6, both groups having gone after "strange flesh" or "pursued unnatural desire" (ESV). Since the sin of Sodom was sexual perversion, "in like manner" the sin of the angels was sexual perversion. If we read Jude a bit further, we see that the ungodly men he is writing of mimic the angels in question with their lascivious behavior:

Likewise also these filthy dreamers defile the flesh, despise dominion, and speak evil of dignities. (Jude 1:8)

Again, this looks to be a reference to Genesis 6, the defilement of all sexual defilements… so terrible and corrupt that God destroyed the world with a global flood. This view is strengthened by the fact that Jude goes on to quote Enoch (Jude 14-15), whose extra-biblical book details the fall, perversions, and imprisonment of the angels in Genesis 6.

One of my favorite commentators writes on Jude 6:

It seems from Scripture that there have been at least two apostasies of angels. One was when Lucifer fell and presumably involved a host of other angelic beings in his rebellion. These fallen angels are not bound at the present time. The devil and his demons are actively promoting war against the LORD *and His people.*

The other apostasy of angels is the one referred to by Jude and also by Peter (2 Pet 2:4). There is considerable difference of opinion among Bible students as to what event is referred to here. What we suggest is a personal viewpoint, not a dogmatic assertion of fact.

We believe that Jude is referring to what is recorded in Gen 6:1–7. The sons of God left their proper estate as angelic beings, came down to the earth in human form, and married the daughters of men. This marital union was contrary to God's order and an abomination to Him. There may be a suggestion in verse 4 that these unnatural marriages produced offspring of tremendous strength and wickedness. Whether or not this is true, it is clear that God was exceedingly displeased with the wickedness of man at this time and determined to destroy the earth with a flood.

There are three objections to this view: (1) The passage in Genesis does not mention angels, but only "sons of God." (2) Angels are sexless. (3) Angels do not marry.

It is true that angels are not specifically mentioned but it is also true that the term "sons of God" does refer to angels in Semitic languages (see Job 1:6; Job 2:1).

There is no Bible statement that angels are sexless. Angels sometimes appeared on earth in human form, having human parts and appetites (Gen 18:2, Gen 18:22; compare Gen 19:1, Gen 19:3-5).

The Bible does not say that angels do not marry but only that in heaven they neither marry nor (are given) in marriage (Mat 22:30).

Whatever historical incident may lie behind verse 6, the important point is that these angels abandoned the sphere which God had marked out for them and are now in chains and in darkness until the time when they will receive their final sentence to perdition.

—William MacDonald, Believer's Bible Commentary, 1992

This perspective on Genesis 6 would also give us another reason why the head covering cannot be hair, since a woman's hair is a part of her beauty, and would contribute to the problem.

I submit it is just as likely as any other interpretation that the command for a woman to wear a head covering when she approaches God "because of the angels" is about protecting the woman (and those around her) from demonic spiritual attack, protecting good angels present in worship from temptation, and rebuking the angels who fell, bound until their judgment.

This may sound quite crazy, but in a day where the church is as powerless as ever, and where even the mention of veiling a woman's head causes "hell" to break loose in the church (literally), maybe there is more warfare involved in this than many think. Perhaps our tendency to skip this section of Scripture only adds to the problem.

It's Not Hair!

Ten Reasons the Christian Head Covering is NOT Hair or Long Hair

And Rebekah lifted up her eyes, and when she saw Isaac, she lighted off the camel. For she had said unto the servant, What man is this that walketh in the field to meet us? And the servant had said, It is my master: therefore she took a vail, and covered herself. (Genesis 24:64-65)

The most popular interpretation today is that the head covering that Paul commands is the hair a woman naturally wears, which is typically longer than a man's. This view does great violence to the Text and actually doesn't make much sense.

Reason 1: The ordinance of head covering is for certain times (v4-6), suggesting a removable covering (v6). It was to be worn during times of prayer and prophecy (or worship). This is not possible with hair. A man (men were instructed not to cover their heads) cannot remove his hair then put it back on when praying is done! The phrase "If a wife (woman) will not" suggests the covering was removable.

Reason 2: There is an obvious distinction between the covering and the hair in verses 5-6. Uncovering and shaving off the hair are obviously two different acts: "*For if the woman be not covered, let her also be shorn*" (v6). This means they cannot be the same.

Reason 3: A woman's hair (length according to the individual) is for her glory. (v15) Part of the purpose of the head covering is to <u>veil</u> this glory, not showcase it. Individual glory is the LAST thing any should want in the Presence of God!

Reason 4: The head covering being hair would create quite a quandary for women who cannot grow "long hair." Can they still pray and prophesy in certain settings with naturally short hair? In the traditional view we are setting forth, regardless of hair length a covering can still be worn.

Reason 5: Woman herself is "the glory of man" (v7) regardless of the length of her hair, therefore she submits and covers herself as man's glory in the Presence of God.

Reason 6: The Greek word for covering in v15 (peribolaion) is different from the one in verses 4-7 (katakaluptō), suggesting Paul was referring to two different coverings…an artificial one and a natural one.

Reason 7: If one substituted "hair" or "long hair" in verse six, it would not make much sense. From the ESV:

"If a wife (woman) will not [have long hair], let her cut her hair short…" She would already have done that! The whole point of that verse is to show the shame of her not covering.

Reason 8: It would be very odd if a woman's symbol of authority in the presence of angels (v10) was one that gave her glory (v15), since the biblical testimony of angelic worship is not glory for angels, but angels showing humility and covering themselves (Isa 6:1-3).

Reason 9: The overall context of verses 14-15. They explain a woman's hair as another example of why she needs an external covering, not the other way around. Her very design as a helper, as the weaker vessel, and with different features than man (including longer hair) says she should cover her head.

Reason 10: The Church agreed with the simplicity and power of this teaching for 1,950 years, from the time of Apostles (v16) through the mid-Twentieth Century (1950-60's). We only began to disobey these precepts on a large scale when feminism hit the West like a tidal wave.

Some Encouragement

All the discomfort surrounding these verses actually demonstrate how "on point" they are. Our resistance shows us how we need to do just what they say. As mentioned previously, we have no problem asking a man to remove his hat in church (or in homes, funerals, during the National Anthem, and other times of reverence). We know it is disrespectful for a man to have his head covered during prayer.

Dear reader, we simply don't like God's plan for women in modern times. We don't like biblical womanhood. The implications of this teaching are difficult for us to accept. Nevertheless, a man's covered head during prayer and prophecy dishonors Christ. Likewise, a woman's uncovered head during prayer and prophecy dishonors man, may be dangerous (angels), and exhibits personal glory before Christ (v4-5, 10, 13).

Is the Word of God Being Blasphemed?

And it came to pass, that when Jehudi had read three or four leaves, he cut it with the penknife, and cast it into the fire that was on the hearth, until all the roll was consumed in the fire that was on the hearth. Yet they were not afraid, nor rent their garments, neither the king, nor any of his servants that heard all these words. (Jeremiah 36:23-24)

In this chapter, I'd like to pose the question asked in the chapter title, and I'd like to use what I think is a relevant example in the area of biblical womanhood.

My favorite dictionary, the Webster 1828 version, defines *Blaspheme* like this:

BLASPHE'ME, *verb transitive* [Gr. The first syllable is the same as in blame, blasme, denoting injury; Latin loedo, loesus; The last syllable is the Gr., to speak.]

1.   To speak of the Supreme Being in terms of impious

irreverence; to revile or speak reproachfully of God, or the Holy Spirit.

2. To speak evil of; to utter abuse or calumny against; to speak reproachfully of.

Blasphemy in Scripture is a great sin. There are many examples, but an instance that comes to mind most often are Jesus' chilling words in Mathew 12:

> *Wherefore I say unto you, All manner of sin and blasphemy shall be forgiven unto men: but the **blasphemy** against the Holy Ghost shall not be forgiven unto men. And whosoever speaketh a word against the Son of man, it shall be forgiven him: but whosoever **speaketh against** the Holy Ghost, it shall not be forgiven him, neither in this world, neither in the world to come. (Matt 12:31-32)*

Blasphemy is in the character of the Beast of Revelation:

> *And they worshipped the dragon which gave power unto the beast: and they worshipped the beast, saying, Who is like unto the beast? who is able to make war with him? **And there was given unto him a mouth speaking great things and blasphemies;** and power was given unto him to continue forty and two months. **And he opened his mouth in blasphemy against God, to blaspheme his name, and his tabernacle, and them that dwell in heaven.** And it was given unto him to make war with the saints,*

*and to overcome them: and power was given him
over all kindreds, and tongues, and nations. And all
that dwell upon the earth shall worship him, whose
names are not written in the book of life of the Lamb
slain from the foundation of the world. If any man
have an ear, let him hear (Rev 13:4-9).*

So blasphemy, or speaking against God, is biblically
unacceptable and extremely dishonorable.

Now, let us read these verses in Titus:

*But speak thou the things which become sound
doctrine: that the aged men be sober, grave,
temperate, sound in faith, in charity, in patience.
The aged women likewise, that they be in behaviour
as becometh holiness, not false accusers, not given
to much wine, teachers of good things; that they
may teach the young women to be sober, to love
their husbands, to love their children, to be discreet,
chaste, keepers at home, good, obedient to their own
husbands, **that the word of God be not blasphemed**.
(Titus 2:1-5)*

Many in our day read Titus chapter two and nod
nostalgically, or maybe even cynically, at the quaint words
therein. "How old fashioned. So 1950's!" But it seems like
there is more at stake. Paul, via the Holy Spirit, taught that
the Word of God is *blasphemed* when young women aren't
taught to "be discreet, chaste, keepers at home, good, and
obedient (submissive, ESV) to their own husbands."

In other words, when women aren't in their proper roles and sphere, the Word of God is reviled (ESV)! This of course would be true for men too. The next verse says, "Young men <u>likewise</u> exhort to be sober minded." (Titus 2:6) But I'd like to put forward a proposition:

Women, even more than men, are given the opportunity to "show" or visibly demonstrate the outworking of Scripture and the power of the Gospel in a transformed life... to be a manifest witness of submission to Christ.

Why do I believe this?

1. The man represents Christ, the woman the church. (Eph 5:23-32) Christ leads but is invisible. The church submits and is VERY visible. Of course a husband is not invisible, but a sure way to tell if his home is orderly is the posture of his wife.
2. Wicked spiritual forces have desired the woman since the beginning (Gen 3, 6:1-8), suggesting her influence in a society.
3. She must cover her head when she prays or prophesies, which is a *visible* symbol that she accepts her role and the authority over her. (1 Cor 11:2-16)
4. The woman is beautiful and is described as the glory of man (1 Cor 11:7). Without question, and by design, she attracts attention much more than the man. Again, she covers her head, in part, to veil her beauty (her glory)! (1 Cor 11:15)

5. Although both male and female are supposed to be modest, a woman's modesty, because of her design, is more prominent. This is reflected in how Scripture speaks of modesty in primarily female terms. (Isa 3:16; Prov 7:10; 1 Tim 2:9; 1 Pet 3:3-5)

Whether we like it or not, the woman is often "on display." What she does or doesn't do and the manner in which she lives is a great indicator of either the presence of the Gospel or its absence.

Whether you agree with my proposition or not, most will see some truth here: *The great temptation in a society is rarely for men to totally abandon manhood. A man knows he must provide and protect; he just needs to be "sober minded" and disciplined. The great temptation is almost always for the woman to leave her sphere, abandon her home, and give the care of her children to others.*

Comfortingly, this teaching against reviling the Word is repeated elsewhere in Scripture in a similar context:

> *"I will therefore that the younger women marry, bear children, <u>guide the house, give none occasion to the adversary to speak reproachfully.</u>" (1 Tim 5:14)*

Apparently, operating in one's assigned sphere or estate in holiness is important:

> *Let as many servants as are under the yoke count their own masters worthy of all honour, that the name of God and his doctrine be not <u>blasphemed</u>. (1 Tim 6:1)*

Paul says this sort of abdication (abandoning assigned roles and responsibilities) causes the Word of God to be blasphemed. But how? I submit this happens in three ways:

1. Blasphemy from Satan

My friend Scott Brown said, "You must understand the motivation behind the hateful wiles of the Devil against homemaking. The roaring lion is seeking to destroy the souls of the next generation. He prefers unprotected homes. Instead of ruling and nurturing their homes, (women) are ruling and nurturing elsewhere." (*Feminine by Design*, p. 64)

Satan speaks evil of God and anything He ordained for His own glory, including creation order and domestic life. The more the devil can speak ill of and disrupt this order, the more cultural and generational damage he can do. All we have to do is look around to see this truth.

2. Blasphemy from Society

Again, Elder Brown said, "Those who choose to be keepers at home will be mocked and belittled. They will be made to feel guilty. They are scolded that they're wasting their lives. They are told they are not making quite enough of themselves." (*Feminine by Design*, p. 63)

Being a "keeper of the home" is not a common aspiration today; in fact, it is ridiculed. How much beauty has been lost because the Word of God and the design of God is *reviled* in this manner?

3. Blasphemy from the Saints… from the Women Themselves

My wife Donna says, "When young women are not trained

to love and submit to their own husbands, they begin to despise God's Word. There is a *hatred* that occurs. This hatred of God's Word is exemplified by the feminist movement which has destroyed the family."

Does anyone doubt that many (if not most) women (even many Christian women!) despise and revile the biblical texts about womanhood?

Like King Jehoiakim in Jeremiah 36, many people, including many Christians, look with utter disdain upon certain Scriptures, especially those that govern home and church life. They cannot bear certain Texts to be read, even in church. Most do not go as far as to have the verses cut from the Bible and burned, as Jehoiakim did to Jeremiah's prophetic words for him, but the scorn and disrespect for Scripture is still there.

Most would agree with me that 1 Corinthians 11:1-16 makes just about everyone's list of hated passages. These and other verses (like 1 Tim 2:11-14 or 1 Cor 14:33-38) are met with real hostility and contempt, and pastors fear to preach them as a result.

Not only are these Texts handled irreverently, but disobeying them results in a *slander* of Scripture. God's Word and those who preach it are accused of being chauvinist, patriarchal (in a negative way), and misogynistic. These *blasphemies* are common now, and accepted by large swaths of culture and Church.

So, is the Word of God being blasphemed?

In my opinion, sadly, yes it is.

The Most Dangerous Attitude I've Ever Seen

And the LORD said unto Moses, I have seen this people, and, behold, it is a stiffnecked people. (Exodus 32:9)

During family worship recently, my wife and I discussed an attitude all too prevalent in the church. A dangerous attitude. In fact, I'm struggling to think of a MORE dangerous attitude. I think this attitude is often (not always) present when considering the ordinance of head coverings.

Studying the Shorter Catechism, our family was working through this question and answer about the LORD's Prayer:

Q.103: For what do we pray in the third request?
A: In the third request (your will be done on earth as it is in heaven) we pray that by His grace God would make us have the capability and the will to know, obey, and submit to His will in everything, as the angels do in heaven.

My wife brought up the subject and described the attitude. This attitude says:

"Yes, that is God's Word. Yes, I acknowledge that His Word is true. I simply choose not to obey it."

When she brought this up, *I trembled.* I immediately began searching my own heart for such rebellion, as she did. Then I thought about the many times I've seen this. I said to her, "I cannot think of a more dangerous attitude than this."

Why?

- Because this sentiment is normally expressed by a professing believer. An atheist etc. would not acknowledge God's Word.
- Because to have such an attitude as a follower of Christ reflects an almost total lack of the fear of the LORD.
- Because this is the exact same attitude that brought the wrath of God upon Israel over and over again, and upon Jerusalem, prophesied by Christ in the New Testament (Fulfilled in 70 AD).
- Because if a professing believer can acknowledge the Truth, but refuse it, where does he/she go from there?

Scripture declares:

For if we go on sinning deliberately after receiving the knowledge of the truth, there no longer remains a sacrifice for sins, but a fearful expectation of judgment, and a fury of fire that will consume the adversaries. Anyone who has set aside the law of Moses dies without mercy on the evidence of two or three witnesses. How much worse punishment, do you think, will be deserved by the one who has trampled underfoot the Son of God, and has profaned the blood of the covenant by which he was sanctified, and has outraged the Spirit of grace? For we know him who said, "Vengeance is mine; I will repay." And again, "The LORD *will judge his people." It is a fearful thing to fall into the hands of the living God. (Heb 10:26-31)*

Oh friends, the LORD declares in so many places, this heart:

Do not now be stiff-necked as your fathers were, but yield yourselves to the LORD and come to his sanctuary, which he has consecrated forever, and serve the LORD your God, that his fierce anger may turn away from you. (2 Chronicles 30:8)

You stiff-necked people, uncircumcised in heart and ears, you always resist the Holy Spirit. As your fathers did, so do you. (Acts 7:51)

Essentially, this attitude *blatantly* resists the Holy Spirit. It grieves Him (Eph 4:30). It makes a mockery of His convicting work (John 16:8) and places the professing believer in the untenable place of boldly acting like an enemy of God.

May I encourage you?

If this book is resonating with you, but you are fearful, **love God through your obedience anyway (John 14:15)**! Realize that an attitude of blatant resistance to Scripture is not only blasphemous, but DANGEROUS.

Dangerous for you. Dangerous for your family. Dangerous for your children. Dangerous for your church.

Forgive me LORD, for surely I've had this same attitude many times before. May Your people beg Your mercy and deliverance from such.

Amen.

A Needed Symbol

But one thing is needful: and Mary hath chosen that good part, which shall not be taken away from her. (Luke 10:42)

At the end of Luke chapter 10, we find Mary and her sister Martha interacting with Jesus. It is a familiar Text to many:

Now it came to pass, as they went, that he entered into a certain village: and a certain woman named Martha received him into her house. And she had a sister called Mary, which also sat at Jesus' feet, and heard his word. But Martha was cumbered about much serving, and came to him, and said, LORD, dost thou not care that my sister hath left me to serve alone? Bid her therefore that she help me. And Jesus answered and said unto her, Martha, Martha, thou art careful and troubled about many things: But one thing is needful: and Mary hath chosen that good part, which shall not be taken away from her. (Luke 10:38-42)

Much has been made of the wisdom of Mary, pausing her domestic service to sit at the feet of the Master. There she "heard his word." I'm praying this book causes many precious sisters to pause and hear the heart of the Master as well.

The Beauty of Womanhood

Please take a moment and read Genesis 2:15-24 and 3:20.

I'm convinced that God's creation, as designed, was beautiful. Imagine the lush, unstained forests, the colors of the meadows and fields, the unspoiled mountains and seas, and the paradise that was the Garden of Eden.

Into this paradise, God, in love, placed the crowning jewels of His creation, Adam and Eve. And God walked among them in the cool of the day, obviously desiring a loving relationship with His children (Gen 3:8).

Woman is the last creature God created, and in my view, He saved the best for last! With all my heart, **I believe that *Woman* was created with beauty in mind, to be delightful inside and out, and has a beautiful purpose given by God!**

If you took the time to read the suggested Scriptures, you'll find that God put Adam in the garden to work it and keep it. Part of man's purpose is to labor. This is how man takes dominion. But man was not complete. God wasn't quite finished. Man could not then and can not now accomplish his dominion purpose without woman. God said, *"It is not good that the man should be alone. I will make him a helper fit for him."* (Gen 2:18, ESV) Here we find the great purpose for Woman, and that great purpose is a part of her beauty:

Woman was formed for man, to be a helper fit for him.

Now, note that after Eve's creation, God was finished! Woman is the last thing God made. *She is the best and brightest stone on the crown of creation, the finishing touch in the mind of God, and designed by God to be a beautifying "corner pillar" fit for a palace* (Ps 144:12).

Indeed, so precious is this pinnacle of beauty, Scripture unfolds a lifetime of care for her. From birth to gray hair, God commands her protection and provision. Not only that, but she is given the privilege to be a mother, the one who literally conceives within her womb and brings human life into the world! What is more beautiful than that? (Gen 3:20)

Dear reader, we know that Satan works to mar and disfigure everything that God created. His desire is to make the beautiful ugly and the ugly seem beautiful. Nowhere is this more apparent in the current culture (and sadly, the contemporary church) than among women. I submit to you that woman, especially the Christian woman, is:

1. **Beautiful** in her role as a daughter of Christ, reflecting our LORD's tenderness and care, His patience and tenacity, His submission to and love for His Father.

2. **Beautiful** in her role as an unmarried servant of the Kingdom, making the mission of her family and the church her priority until she weds.

3. **Beautiful** in her role as wife and mother, taking up her role in the picture of Christ and His church (Eph 5), exalted in her role as the submitted bride.

4. **Beautiful** in her role as a mentor and discipler of her children, pouring consistently and exhaustingly into her progeny day after day, crying aloud for them in the secret place as only a mother can.

5. **Beautiful** when she models modesty, rejecting the examples of the world and witnessing to all of creation the Christian virtues of propriety, meekness, and humility.

A Needed Symbol

The head covering symbolizes all that is strong and anointed about biblical womanhood. The head covering is gentle, feminine, meek, quiet, tender, and yet filled with the authority of the Sword of the Spirit. It is a powerful demonstration that the wearer, a daughter of Eve, refuses to follow the aforementioned in her independence and susceptibility to deception because she has been transformed by Jesus.

The head covering is a subversive symbol in modern times that shouts loudly into the physical and spiritual world that Christ is King and His Word is *"quick, and powerful, and sharper than any two-edged sword, piercing even to the dividing asunder of soul and spirit, and of the joints and marrow, and is a discerner of the thoughts and intents of the heart"* (Heb 4:12).

Consider how times have changed since the Western church rejected the head covering. Think about what has happened to marriage, home-making, the discipling of children, modesty, sexuality, submission, church roles, and meek and quiet spirits. Consider modern men as well, mostly passive, addicted to sports, and faltering in their discipleship and breadwinner duties.

Yes, this sounds awfully old fashioned, and no, the loss of the head covering didn't cause all this. But its loss is symptomatic of a wider rejection of the Word of God.

Think with me. If women continued to cover their heads when they approached God, do you think there would be as much immodesty as there is now? If women continued to cover their heads when they worshipped, do you think there would be as many women pastors, bishops, apostles, and chief apostles as is popular today? If women continued to cover their heads when they approached God, do you think there would be as much "strong delusion" and Jezebel-like rebellion and destruction in the church?

No, I'm not blaming women for all of society's ills. Those who know me know I'm much harder on men! But in many ways, women make or break a nation, a church, and a family. The influence of a woman is powerful, whether she is godly or not. Therefore we need godly women now more than ever before.

The contemporary church NEEDS this symbol.

We need the head covering more than we realize. It isn't nearly as "small" as we think. The good news is that it's happening! Small groups of believers are returning to it. Its recovery on a large scale would change much in the church and in the home almost overnight. God would bless us richly if we simply, and with child-like faith, obeyed the Word of God.

May the Church of Jesus Christ do just that.

Amen.

Final Thoughts

But be ye doers of the word, and not hearers only,
deceiving your own selves. (James 1:22)

When it comes to head covering, the western church applies a very selective hermeneutic. In fact, I think 1 Corinthians in general causes us to "blink" on several occasions.

For example, in 1 Corinthians 14, many conservative Christians would hold to the prohibitions against women speaking in the church (vv34-37) but see the regulations concerning prophecy and tongues in the church as irrelevant in these "closed-cannon" times (vv1-33, 39-40). On the other hand, many in non-denominational and pentecostal traditions essentially ignore the verses on women not speaking in church, but hold vigorously to the gifts of prophecy and tongues. In just one chapter, we can see a break down of *Sola Scriptura* across a wide section of the church.

And then there are God's commands concerning church discipline. In 1 Corinthians 5 we see a man excommunicated for willful, perverse sin. Do you know of any church that has excommunicated a sinning, unrepentant member? So either we are very holy OR very negligent as it relates to church discipline. Very few churches even HAVE a policy on church discipline. Maybe it's bad for business?

First Corinthians 11 is no different. Every protestant church and pastor I know would teach the instructions concerning the LORD's Table as written in 1 Corinthians 11:17-34, and would do so changing nothing, eliminating nothing, and calling for obedience to all. But the vast, vast majority would assign a cultural hermeneutic to the verses right above them which teach and defend head covering.

Biblical schizophrenia!

Seriously, I pray this short book has been a blessing to you. Whether you adopt the practice of head covering or not, I pray at least you've enjoyed this study, and aren't in any way offended.

As a pastor, my job is to love God's people. Dear reader, I love you. But more importantly, Jesus loves you.

In my opinion, there are many areas of reformation needed in the modern church. I believe we need to *Reclaim the Gospel, Reestablish Holiness, Reform the Family, Ready the Church through Stewardship, and Restore Trust in the Church and Her Leaders.*[1]

---

1. I wrote about these areas in my book, *The Playbook: Five Strategic Plays to Restore the Prophetic Voice of the Church in America.* You can find it at CRCChesapeake.org/the-playbook.

But I also believe that everything God gave His church is important, including the head covering. Sadly, had we maintained this holy ordinance and all it symbolized, I doubt the church and family would be in the position in which we currently find ourselves. Symbols are powerful.

May the LORD restore our trust in Scripture, and enable us, by the Holy Spirit, to obey.

A Female Perspective

Yet hear the word of the LORD, O ye women, and let your ear receive the word of his mouth, and teach your daughters wailing, and every one her neighbour lamentation. (Jeremiah 9:20)

Considering the above verse, I once jokingly said to a sister, who was known to be a prayer warrior but not covering at the time, "You have not truly wailed until you have veiled." I suggested that during her private prayer time that she try it. She later came to me with her usual enthusiasm, covered and overjoyed! "Thank you! I didn't know!" Now that doesn't really tell the reader how it "feels" and I have come to realize that words really cannot express the feeling. But I can say that there is an internal comfort that comes with obeying even the "smallest" commandment.

I had always thought I was a graceful, feminine woman, but I was wrong. Covering "softened" me in a manner that

I did not expect or thought was needed. I always thought I was a "ladylike" woman. I could take care of myself if I needed to but I was not manly. I was shocked to find out just how "manly" I really was. I lead a dance team at our church, and young boys would dance with us sometimes. I had no problem choreographing masculine moves for them. But as I started to become more feminine, I could not think of anything to choreograph for them.

As a parent, I always want my children to quickly obey. I also want them to obey everything I say. It does not matter whether it is something "small" or "big." I expect obedience. I do not always follow-up their disobedience with a punishment. Sometimes the natural punishment is punishment enough, things like the scraped knee or missing a fun activity. As I grow in Christ, I have learned that just as my liberty has grown, so has my restriction. I am constrained and bound to follow laws and statutes that I sometimes do not fully understand. Nevertheless I fully understand that they have been given. I think this sentiment may be true for many as it relates to the head covering. God has spoken on the subject. We should simply follow Him.

I have stated and continue to believe that many women who are afraid to cover are mostly afraid of other women. They do not typically fear the woman who is unaware of this Scripture, nor the woman who believes that head covering was cultural. Most women who are afraid to cover are afraid of the women who know we should cover, but they refuse to do so and do not want to be reminded of it. This is the group that will break up friendships over a piece of cloth on your head. This is the group that will approach you and say, "All of that is not necessary" and say it with anger and intimidation. This is sad for all involved and totally misses the point:

Jesus is worthy of obedience and
His Word is perfect and for our good!

Ladies, perhaps you've had similar experiences. When I cover:

- I am humbled as I remember God's Word and creation order
- I am empowered as I remember I receive spiritual (God) and physical (my husband) protection
- I am softened as I remember I am under authority
- I am made lowly as I style my hair until it is cute, then cover it
- I am isolated in God's Presence

This "isolation" I am referring to is a wonderful thing. During times of prayer (private or public) a veil blocks out the outside. It can really feel like a closed room, where only you and the LORD are present, and I say this as a mother with a four and six-year-old! It is what I imagine the Old Testament priest must have felt like entering into the Most Holy Place... but even better. Perhaps it is how Mary felt sitting at the Master's feet.

The veil separating God's people from Him is torn; we now have direct access to our LORD, both male and female. Hallelujah!

Because of Christ dying on the cross and His glorious resurrection, we can commune with Him... but how often do you have that physical feeling? Do I always have this level of closeness to the Master? No, but I now have it more often than not, and the head covering has been an important part of that. What a blessing!

Be strong ladies. God is for you, not against you!

Donna L. McLeod

Epilogue: Words of Thanks

First, I'd like to thank our LORD Jesus, for continuing to teach and instruct His church. Truly, He is Alpha and Omega, the First and the Last. (Rev 1:11) He is the One in the midst of the seven golden candlesticks, and He who holds the seven stars in His right hand. (Rev 1:13, 16) He is He that liveth, and was dead, and is alive forevermore… He who has the keys of hell and death. (Rev 1:18)

He is absolute LORD *of the Church, and everything else.*
To Him alone be glory and honor, Amen.

Next, I want to thank my precious wife, who came to the conclusion that the head covering is a perpetual ordinance before I did! She makes biblical womanhood so easy for me to understand. She obeys God quicker than any woman I've ever seen. Thank you Donna. I love you.

I'd also like to offer appreciation to the brothers and

sisters I've learned from on the Internet:

- Jeremy Gardiner (HeadCoveringMovement.com)
- Greg Gordon (SermonIndex.net)
- Zac Poonen (CFCIndia.com)
- K.P. Yohannan (HeadCoveringMovement.com/
  christian-covering-media/free-e-book-head-
  coverings-by-k-p-yohannan)
- Jessica Roldan (Truth at Home on You Tube)
- April Cassidy (The Peaceful Wife on You Tube)

And finally, I'd like to thank my precious church. Thank you all for being so willing to honor God and His Word. Thank you for allowing me to simply teach Scripture. Thank you for your submission to the Holy Text, and your desire to be a "doer, not a hearer only." Love you all.

Carlton C. McLeod

Appendix:
Encouraging Feedback!

But he said, Yea rather, blessed are they that hear the word of God, and keep it. (Luke 11:28)

Over the last many months, we've received many encouraging letters and emails from precious saints who took the time to share. We are deeply humbled and grateful. God is restoring His church everywhere! I've included so many of these thoughtful comments below, frankly, to encourage those of you struggling with the fear of man as it relates to this beautiful ordinance. You aren't alone, even in these modern times! There were also many phone calls from around the country that encouraged us greatly. Thank you!

Brothers and Sisters, stand strong in the LORD! He makes NO mistakes! His Word is perfect!

The law of the LORD is perfect, converting the soul: the testimony of the LORD is sure, making wise the simple. The statutes of the LORD are right, rejoicing the heart: the commandment of the LORD is pure, enlightening the eyes. The fear of the LORD is clean, enduring for ever: the judgments of the LORD are true and righteous altogether. More to be desired are they than gold, yea, than much fine gold: sweeter also than honey and the honeycomb. (Psalms 19:7-10)

Solus Christus,
Carlton C. McLeod

Dear Dr. McLeod,

I wanted to thank you for your excellent sermon on "Head Coverings" recently posted on YouTube. Your clear teaching and the convincing manner in which you handled what can often be a sensitive subject is to be commended. As an Orthodox Christian priest (Orthodox Church in America), even though I pastor in a very ancient and traditional church, we still struggle with keeping this most worthy practice of women wearing head coverings. Thank you for your thoughtful words on this subject.

Rev. Thomas S.

Thank you for the message. We are missionaries in South Dakota and we also believe in the head covering. Please continue preaching the truth.

Liz R

Greetings brothers and sisters of CRCC,

My wife and I were extremely blessed by the anointed message by Dr. McLeod about head coverings. It was a passage we struggled with and were wavering in the LORD's clear message to His church until Dr. McLeod exegetically broke it down verse by verse. We long to do the will of our LORD and as Bishop McLeod stated, we must "let the Scriptures change [us]."

May the LORD continue to pour His Spirit on your congregation and we look forward to our worshiping Him together forever.

Jermaine P.

Dear Brother Carlton,

I just viewed your message on the head covering in 1 Cor. 11 and say "Amen" to all you shared. I am an anabaptist pastor and appreciate your willingness to accept the truth of the Word. I'm curious how your congregation has adopted and applied the precept of the covering? Women will truly find the blessing of God in obedience to this ordinance. God bless and keep on keeping on.

Marlin B.

I applaud and bless you greatly for your sermon on the head covering. It is refreshing to see other churches have an honest, biblical conversation about this subject. All the women in our churches wear the head covering. GOD bless you real good!!

Aaron H.

I want to thank you for your message. It blessed me to see someone approach God's Word with the desire to hear what God is saying that supersedes the desire to hear what you want to hear. Thank you for properly handling the Word of God and not allowing fear of man to keep you from preaching the truth!

I am a member of a congregation that teaches and practices the head covering (Mennonite). I regret that we have attached other baggage to this Biblical teaching. But it was refreshing to be reminded that this is a Biblical teaching, not a Mennonite teaching. It is also refreshing to see (contrary to what I am told sometimes) that other individuals and congregations besides Mennonites want to know and live by what God teaches in His Word. In the same breath I admit that many of us Mennonites are not doing as well with that as we often say we are. Your message and your personal example challenged me to be willing to listen and change when God shows me through His Word where I need to change.

Again, thanks! Keep preaching the Word of God! And encourage your congregation that they have other brothers and sisters in America who are applying this teaching to their lives!

Blessings,
Keith N.

Dear Sir,
I watched your message on the head covering and was really blessed by your honesty and integrity. Love what you are doing brother. I am a pastor among the anabaptist people who are losing their appreciation for the head covering.

    L.B.

I was so blessed to hear your sermon on the head covering. Sometimes the truth is uncomfortable, and having to step back and examine the Word is scary. Thank you for stepping out and being vulnerable. God bless you and your congregation!

    Kendra M.

Dear Man of God,
I'm a 36-year-old Pastor of a small Baptist church. One of my dear Mennonite friends forwarded a link to the sermon that you preached on head coverings in May 2014. Wow brother… You preached the Word! You rightly divided the Word of Truth, and gave the most God-honoring and well thought out, sermon on this topic. I've personally been convinced of the head covering for about 10 years.

My wife has not been as on board, but has not fought it hard either. We watched your video together. She became so convicted, she paused the video and said she felt like crying because of how she had resisted this clear call in

Scripture. There has been a real change in her since then. God bless you Man of God! You are a BLESSING!

Corey F.

Please, please forward this message to the pastor who taught on head coverings. First I'd like to say how much we who want to know truth appreciate your courage and willingness to teach something so risky in today's culture. My husband and I left a traditional church after 20 years to reestablish the practice of covering and submission to male authority which is no longer taught in most secular Christian churches. Thank you, thank you for your bravery in teaching such truth in the face of hatred towards God's order for mankind. Blessings to you and those who choose to follow God's Word regardless of the culture. Love, love, love this sermon and will be sharing it with those women who have open hearts to hear truth.

Sincerely,

Leighanna Y.

Thank you for your sermon. I was at a fellowship and one of the ladies mentioned your video was shown to her Bible study group. Many of the group began to understand head covering and why her family chose to cover. However, I am getting ahead of myself.

I can tell you I began covering off and on in March of 2013 and in May '13 covered all the time. For me it has been a struggle, but I know the LORD wants this of me.

I have been 'transforming' for a few years and in those years I have watched my children transform. My daughter is now baptized, my oldest son, though not saved, shares Scripture with me often, and my youngest son actually talks to me. At the same time I have watched my unsaved husband pull away from me. It started with my dressing modestly, wearing skirts all the time, and then I started to cover my head. Oh how he did not want that and even though I would share Scripture with him and explain why I felt this was what the LORD wanted of me, he pulled further from me. Many times hateful things would be said to me.

Last month in a fellowship group, the women began discussing their head covering trials and encouraging me with my marriage. One of the women mentioned the video of your sermon that was used in her Bible study and thought maybe that would be of help like it was to those in their group. The next day she emailed me the link and I sat next to my husband and said would you please watch this with me. He did!

At the end of the video he surprised me. He said he was wrong about covering and understood why I cover and that from now on I am to cover my head. Though he is still unsaved your sermon opened his heart up to some of the Gospel and helped him understand why I am the way I am.

Thank you for being able to preach what the Gospel says about head covering and being honest about your biases. I look forward to watching more of your sermons, especially ones on family and marriage. God Bless You!

Janice R.

I just want to say AMEN! to your sermon on head coverings. I will be praying for your church. I was raised in a Catholic church until my Dad passed and Mom married an atheist. I lived in a sinful, culturally acceptable way. I got pregnant out of wedlock and came to the LORD in fear as most of us do when it is all too much. I married the father and moved (to a different state). I joined our very small Mennonite church 17 years ago. I started to wear a covering when I quit smoking 15 years ago after really studying 1 Cor. 11 on my own. My church never pressured me to. The LORD's Word did.

Sister K. W.

Carlton, I bless the LORD Jesus for His ministry in you. I always look forward to hear what God has been speaking to you. I happened to get turned to your message on the prayer veiling of the Christian wife and was blessed to hear your teaching which has been my heart as well. May you find grace to keep preaching the heart of God to the Body of Christ. May you find fresh wind of the Spirit and courage to walk this world in holiness and purity as we await the soon return of our King, Jesus the Messiah.

Unto Him (Jesus) be all glory Honor and Authority forever!! (Eph 4:15)

Roy W.

Brother McLeod,

This past Sunday in our Conservative Mennonite Church, we watched your sermon on the head covering as our normal Sunday sermon. Our church practices daily wearing of the head covering, however we are seeing more and more Mennonite churches put the covering on the table these days. Anyway, your sermon was so much more than just a sermon on the head covering; it was a true blessing to watch and it had the whole church laughing and talking about it for some time, even during the Brotherhood meeting we had later that night. I have also shared the video with others outside my church, those who would disagree with the head covering. I cannot imagine giving this sermon in a large church that does not practice this. Talking with some brothers it was mentioned that we have had visiting preachers give a head covering sermon before, however hearing a sermon from "one of you" about something you currently do, seems not to be as effective for some reason as your sermon…which was and is done by "someone else" (and knowing it was given to loved ones who do not cover).

Amazing! God has blessed you with a true leader's heart. I commend your boldness to preach God's Word the way it is and in such a way that God's Word "works" to convict and chasten us back to His will and submission to Him. This is the purpose of His Word. I just wanted to share my gratitude and let you know your sermon has touched many hearts and minds. Blessings in Christ's Name.

Doug B.

We listen from afar, up in Lancaster county, PA. The teaching is what we have been hungry for (we are New Englanders that just relocated on faith following Christ Jesus). We have 5 children, and interestingly enough started listening to the sermons online via the one about head coverings. Thank you for preaching and teaching with integrity humility and grace.

All our blessings, your brothers and sisters in Christ,
The O'Neill Family

God Bless you Sir! I recently heard your sermon on YouTube in relation to the head covering or the Christian Woman's Veiling. I grew up Baptist in NC and I later left the Baptist church and became Mennonite for many of the same reasons that you preached about in relation to the modern day movement of negating Scripture based upon societal norms. This message blessed me so much.

Clifton K.

Brother McLeod,
Our family just watched your message on Youtube: *Head Coverings: History, Context, and Exegesis.* Wow! What a blessing! We appreciated your spirit and message. My wife has recently started wearing a head covering although our church background teaches the hair is the covering. Many of the things you said we have journeyed through ourselves

in our research. Thank you for your clear Scriptural teaching. God bless you and your ministry.

In Christ,
Stephen W.

Just wanted to say I appreciated your faithfulness to God and His Word when I listened to this sermon. I have often wondered why mainstream Christianity refuses to accept God's Word as it is written and comes up with excuses as to why we do not have to obey its leading.

Thank you,
Troy J.

I just watched your exegesis of 1 Cor 11: 2-16 on You Tube and it was excellent. I was so encouraged to hear that you went into your study of the passage feeling as if it was cultural, and Scripture spoke and you left the study transformed by it. I live in KY and have been practicing head covering for 3 years now. I am the only one in my church who does, but sermons like yours are confirmation to what I as a layperson have read, and prayed about in a passage the Holy Spirit led me to and illuminated for me, and convicted me personally to follow. I have also wondered for the past 3 years why our church (I am in the reformed Southern Baptist faith tradition) adheres to the teaching in 1 Timothy 2, but doesn't see the parallel to this Scripture.

Janelle T.

I just listened to your hour-long message on head coverings and the roles of women and men. PTL!!! In our Church Fellowship we practice head coverings, the LORD's Supper on a weekly basis, and the biblical roles of women and men in the Church. Some consider us "Plymouth Brethren" but we take no name other than Believers in Jesus Christ and believe in the inerrant Word of God. My question to you after a WONDERFUL message: have any of the women, including your wife, heeded and are now wearing head coverings?

In Him,
Wanda

I am writing this note in response to the sermon you preached in the Spring of 2014 about the head covering. My husband and I listened to your sermon via You Tube. We were challenged and blessed by it. You handle the Word of God very reverently and are very careful in how you interpret it, knowing that you will be held accountable for this. Praise God! God has blessed you with boldness. Wow, we need more men like you in our world.

We are part of the Mennonite church and I grew up covering my head. I appreciated how you explained that the command was not just for the culture of that day but it applies today. I have wondered if it was indeed only for the Corinthians so your explanation was refreshing.

God bless you!
Emily S.

Dear Sir,

Your message on the women's head covering is the most thorough and enlightening that I have heard on the subject. I am an Independent Baptist, and the only lady who covers in our church. I would love to share your message with others, but we believe the King James Bible is the only true Word of God. I have told The LORD that I would not share anything that does not use the KJV. Would it be possible for you to do your sermon again using only the KJV or to make a booklet on the subject using the KJV? I know this is asking a lot, but your understanding of the Scripture is spot on. Please consider doing this. I believe you could be of great help to many ladies.

 Thank you,
 Penny S.

Dr. McLeod,

We had to write and thank you for your sermon on head covering. My wonderful husband and I live in northern Maine with our four children (with two more on the way). Where we live there are many purpose-driven Baptist churches and Catholic churches and none teaching Truth on any of the subjects you touched on in this sermon. The LORD put it on our hearts to really read and study these Scriptures a couple months ago and we decided that I would start covering each day. In a very close-knit community we have received lots of looks and snickers (mostly from church attenders out in the community).

Looking online for someone speaking truth we found your wife's testimony on the Head Covering Movement website and then found your sermon. Your wife's words really helped to encourage me. My husband and I watched your sermon together with our children and the whole time we were nodding along saying AMEN!! Thank you for speaking hard Truths! It seems, in our area anyway, that we are getting away from Scripture as it is written and it was so refreshing to hear your sermon and drink from the well.

Bless you for your words and for standing strong and speaking Truth.

In His Light and Love,
Goose and Gillian

I would first of all like to say thank you for the message that was posted from Calvary Revival Church Chesapeake on your YouTube channel. I know the topic of head coverings can become a very tough subject to tackle, especially for a congregation that may not be all on board with the idea. I thought Carlton McLeod did an excellent job in presenting the Scriptures in a straightforward manner. I attend a small chapel where our elders and the majority of women in our assembly gathering practice a head covering of some sort. Some do not and I have had conversations with others who do not wear them for the "right reasons" (Scriptural reasons).

It was so exciting to see someone speak from 1 Corinthians 11 to a group of believers who were not necessarily practicing what is taught in that passage. Thank you for sharing this message and the reminder that despite what our culture might say, the Word of God must be taught and adhered to.

Joe C.

I listened to your sermon on head coverings. You are right on with the Scriptures. I was convicted about wearing a head covering and have been wearing one for 2 years now. I pray the women in your congregation humbled themselves and have started to wear a head covering. The church has fallen far away and to speak up on covering today is not very popular. Thank you for speaking the truth.

Carol M.

Good Evening,

I have literally just finished watching your YouTube sermon on the head covering. As a 41 year old male who has been raised in an Anabaptist Fellowship and continues to be a member, I am humbled. As you spoke, by the power of GOD, on a subject that you were clearly not comfortable talking on, I realize that I have nearly forgotten the REAL reason why the sisters wear the covering. We just do it and move on.

Blessings to you and I encourage you to continue to speak the BIBLICAL truth and trust the LORD for strength and courage!!!
Chad K.

Dear Dr. McLeod,
I was recently blessed to watch your message on the Christian woman's head covering and I was curious to hear how it has worked out practically in your church. Has your church largely accepted it as doctrinal truth or has it been an isolated few who have stepped forward in faith on this issue? Your courage as a pastor to be honest with the Sacred Word of God demonstrates true humility before Him. To me, I understand true repentance to be, not just turning from sin, but also a complete renunciation of self and all its rights for defending itself against God and His brilliantly clear demands upon us. When we stand before Him on judgment day, I believe that it will be ever so clear who our greatest loyalty was to - Him or Self. God bless you in this!
Caleb W.

Pastor, I cannot honor you enough. I know what that sermon on the covering cost you, and the Goliath you stand against. However, it is the truth, and for that, I say THANK YOU!!! I am at work and I can't type much, but thank you for telling the truth no matter who or what doesn't like it. I have struggled with the covering for 25 years but God won't let me go from it. Please pray that I will have the anointing and courage to do so, all the time, because I am commanded to "pray always" so I feel I should be covered always. I stand with you. Those Scriptures you tackled, on the woman being silent also, no one deals with today. I know the LORD is pleased. If you need a sister to come and give you some "amens" I would be glad too!!!

Much love in Yeshua,
Sherry C.

❧

I just today heard your message on head covering and want to say what a marvelous sermon that was. You are brave to tackle it. Our family agrees with what you had to say about head coverings. I hope your congregation hears the truth and will follow the Scripture obediently.

Barbara P.

❧

I am a brother in Christ from Northern Indiana. I recently listened to your message about head coverings and was blown away. My response was like David's, "My heart standeth in awe of Thy Word." I appreciate so much, not only the subject matter, but even more encouraging is the way in which the Word of God was handled. Thank you so much for handling the Word with such honesty and fear (in a good sense). I am greatly encouraged, and wanted to encourage you brother to continue to stand on every Word of God, and to continue to earnestly contend for the faith that was once delivered to the saints.

God bless you and thank you!

Ryan M.

Thank you for the message on head coverings. I have shared much of the same with our small fellowship in Ontario, Canada. In our fellowship, acceptance of head coverings for women is a part of our membership covenant. Some of our community, in hearing your sermon, wondered what response you have received in your own congregation, as well as from the wider Christian community. Have others in your church embraced this teaching?

Steve G.

Dear Dr. McLeod,

Recently I was on the Head Covering Movement website and they had posted your video on head coverings. It was great and I was so glad the LORD led me to hear you. I believe in this but in my world no one practices it. I was so blessed by your sermons on womanhood and others also. Your sermons on the integrated church as well as the head covering sermon was like warm honey on my soul!

I have been praising the LORD for finding your sermons and can't thank you enough for preaching the truth of God's Word and standing strong when is not convenient in this day and age to do so.

Joni R.

Dear Pastor,

I am presently preaching through 1 Corinthians and am scheduled to preach 11:2-16 next week. I've been mulling over that text for a long time now. Having arrived at a similar conclusion to you, one of the ladies in my church just sent me your sermon. I was moved to tears twice, feeling overwhelmed by God's kindness, at least in part because I know there is another brother who has also newly taught this text with a consistent hermeneutic. I've not taught this before to our congregation, and I'm greatly encouraged by your tone, content, and humble example.

Thank you.

Pastor Jacob Reaume, Harvest Bible Chapel, Waterloo Region Ontario

About the Author

D
r. Carlton McLeod is a native of Columbia, South Carolina, but grew up in Maryland. He has been married to his beautiful wife Donna since 1992, and they have three children: Dori, Aryanna, and Jonathan. Carlton lives in Chesapeake, Virginia.

After serving in the United States Navy for nearly twelve years as both officer and enlisted, Carlton planted his church in 1997, resigning from the military in 2002.

Carlton serves as the Senior Pastor of Calvary Revival Church Chesapeake, and currently has the honor to serve other pastors in the United States and the Caribbean as a jurisdictional bishop in Calvary Alliance of Churches and Ministries.

His previous books and tracts include:
- *Jesus is Enough: One Church's Transformation from Spiritual Consumers to More Mature Followers of Christ*
- *The Playbook: Five Strategic Plays to Restore the Prophetic*

Voice of the Church in America
- *Imagine: Hope in a World of Hurt*

You can find information on Carlton, his books, and the church he serves at:

CRCChesapeake.org
D6Reformation.org
Twitter: @ccmcleod

Made in United States
Troutdale, OR
04/16/2024

19218760R00060